Biff, Chip & Kipper

Stories and Activities

Series created by
Roderick Hunt & Alex Brychta

Activities written by
Isabel Thomas

OXFORD
UNIVERSITY PRESS

Tips for reading

Sharing stories is one of the best ways to help children learn to read. The two *Biff, Chip and Kipper* stories featured in this book are a springboard to fun activities that will help your child to practise sounds, letters and early reading skills at home.

The best way to encourage your child is to offer lots of praise. When they complete the book, help them to find the matching reward sticker. Then, when they get to the end of the book, they can complete the 'well done' certificate on page 32.

Making learning fun

Both stories have familiar characters and settings to build your child's vocabulary and knowledge about the world. The themed activities provide opportunities to talk about the stories and will help your child to develop important skills for reading and writing.

You'll also find ideas for games and activities to continue the fun after you've finished each section.

Children learn best when they are having fun. Find a time to read with your child when they are not too tired or distracted. At **Read with Oxford Stage 1** children should be able to concentrate on activities for about 5-10 minutes.

Enjoying the activities

Each time you return to the book, share the story again before you start the activities. Children enjoy re-reading stories and this gentle reminder helps to build their confidence and will make the activities fun and easier to complete.

Before reading

Read the title of the story together and look at the pictures. Ask your child what they think the story is about.

Before you read the stories, show your child these letters. Say the sounds they make.

d o n a e t m u f b
s p g c k r h l

You can listen to the letter sounds at **oxfordowl.co.uk**

Practise blending the sounds to make these words. Say the sounds in each word, then blend the sounds together to make the word (e.g. *B-i-ff, Biff*).

Story 1
on Dad
get Mum

Story 2
bus stop
hop bag run
got ran lap

Tricky words

'Tricky words', or 'common exception words', are words which do not follow the phonics rules that your child will be learning in school. Your child may need help with these tricky words and names. Say them together before you start reading.

Story 1
go

Story 2
the to no
was that

Floppy

Chip

Kipper

When you come across these words in the stories, remind your child they are tricky words that they need to recognise. Encourage your child to have a go at saying them out loud. Say the word for them if they struggle.

Oxford Owl

The Oxford Owl website is packed full of resources to help support your child's learning at home. Visit **oxfordowl.co.uk** to find more activities, free eBooks, information on the **Read with Oxford Stages** and other practical advice to help your child progress with reading.

Enjoy the stories!

Get Dad

Written by **Roderick Hunt**

Illustrated by **Alex Brychta**

Go on, Dad!

Get Biff.

Go on, Dad!

Get Chip.

Go on, Dad!

Get Kipper.

Go on, Mum!

Get Dad!

 Find a butterfly in each picture.

Sound play

Now that you have finished reading the story, retell it in your own words.

1 **Colour** the pictures.
Choose a sound sticker for each picture.

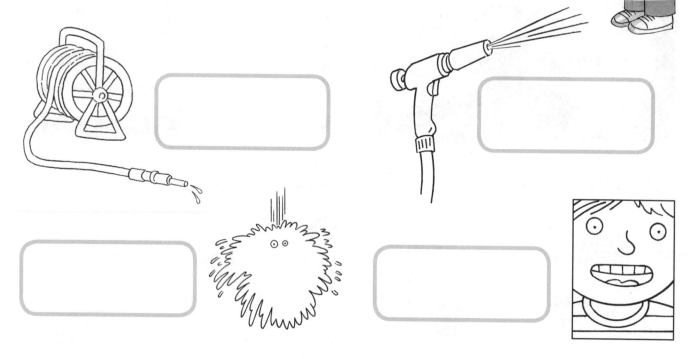

sssssssssh   **splash**   **eeeeek**   **drip drip**

2 **Trace** the words. **Read** the words and make each noise.

tap   pat   puff

rat-a-tat

3 **Look** at the pictures. **Say** the names. **Draw** a line to join the ones that sound the same.

4 **Colour** all the pictures. **Circle** all the things that begin with the sound /s/.

5 **Trace** the letter. **Write** the letter.

Try this!

Sing a funny nursery rhyme together. Ask your child to tell you any words that rhyme.

Sounds at the beginning of words

How many different ways did people get wet in the story? What did the children like about the game?

1 **Say** the letter sounds on the buckets. **Draw** a line from each picture to the right letter.

2 **Say** the names of the pictures in each bucket. **Choose** the right letter sticker to put on each bucket.

3 **Blend** the sounds together to say the words. **Write** the missing letters.

g e t   __et

d a d   __ad

h o t   __ot

t i p   __ip

m u m   __um

Try this!

Choose a sound. Go on a treasure hunt for things that start with that sound.

Sounds at the end of words

How did Dad feel when he got wet? What do you think happened after he got wet?

1 **Colour** the picture. **Use** red for things that end with the sound /**g**/. **Use** blue for things that end with the sound /**t**/.

2 **Write** the letter **g** or **t** at the end of each word.

 le __   shir __   fro __

 ca __   do __    ha __

10

3 **Trace** the last letter of each word.
Join the words that end with the same sound.

can   cap

nip   pin

tin   top

4 **Say** the words. **Listen** to the sound at the end
of each word. **Circle** the odd one out.

Try this! Lay out four objects, e.g. a pen, a toy dog, a cup and a hat. Write
the letters **t**, **g**, **p** and **n** on pieces of paper. Ask your child to
move each letter next to the object that ends with that sound.

Sounds in the middle of words

Do you like playing games with water? What else do you do to cool down when it's hot?

1 **Say** the words. **Write** the missing letters.

 m __ p

 d __ g

 s __ n

 d __ p

 h __ n

2 **Join** the words with the same sound in the middle.

hot   get   rip   Dad   pot

sad   run   tip   pet   Mum

3 Circle the right words to tell the story.

It is hot / top.

Biff gets pet / wet.

Dad has bun / fun.

Mum tips / sips **it.**

Mum gets Dad / mad.

Try this!

Collect 10 pebbles (or pieces of paper). Write the letters **s, a, t, p, i, n, m, d, g** and **o** in marker pen. Arrange three stones to make a word, e.g. *s-a-t*. Ask your child to leave the middle stone where it is and change the other letters to make new words. Try with a different starting word, e.g. *d-o-g* or *p-i-n*.

Letter sound practice

Try not to get wet!

Play the game. Find a counter each. Take it in turns to roll a dice. When you land on a letter, **say** the sound. If you land on a splash, **miss** a go.

Try this! → Choose a sound. In the garden, pretend to splash things that start with that sound!

Each time you finish the game, have a reward sticker.

Handwriting practice

Trace the letters. **Say** the sounds. **Write** the letters and then **add** a sticker that starts with the sound.

a _____

t _____

p _____

i _____

n _____

m _____

d _____

g _____

Page 6

eeeeek   splash   drip drip   sssssssh

Page 8

b   m   d   f

Page 15

Pages 16-17

Pages 16-17

Page 23

laptop   **dog**   **bag**   **bus**   **hat**

Pages 28-29

Page 31

Page 32

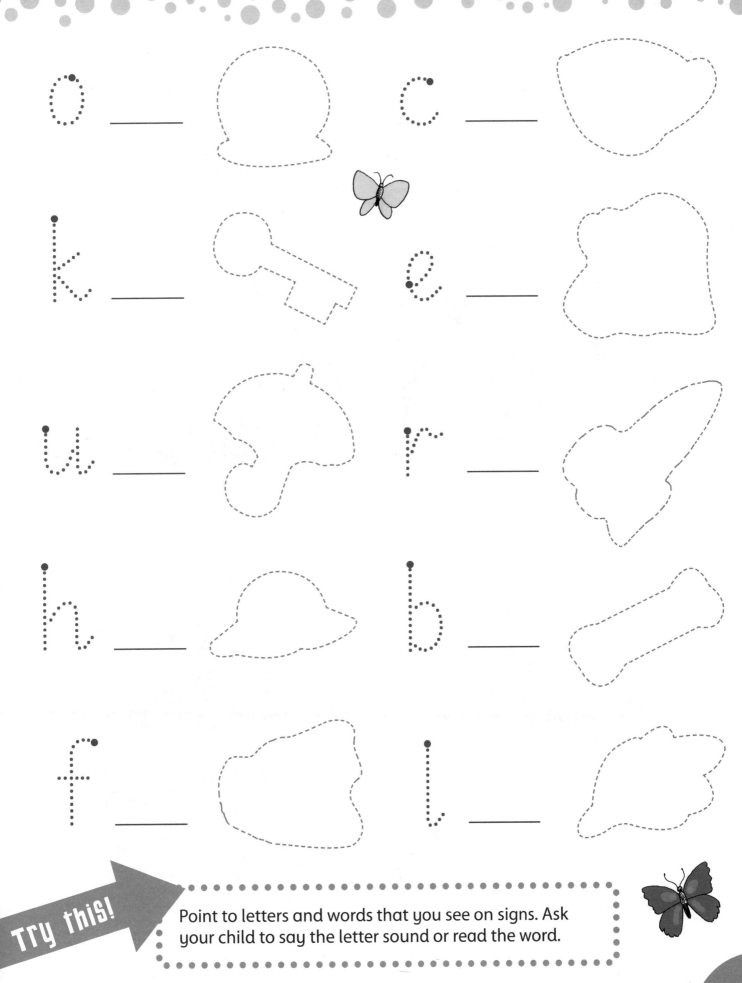

o ___

c ___

k ___

e ___

u ___

r ___

h ___

b ___

f ___

l ___

Point to letters and words that you see on signs. Ask your child to say the letter sound or read the word.

The Bag on the Bus

Written by **Roderick Hunt**
Illustrated by **Nick Schon**

Mum and Biff got off the bus.

Mum's bag was on the bus.

Mum ran and Biff ran.

Dad and Kipper ran.

Chip and Floppy ran.

Mum got to the bus stop.

Mum got her bag back...

Mum got her laptop back.

Find six pigeons in the pictures.

19

Letter sounds

What did Mum leave on the bus? How did she feel?

1 **Say** the letter sounds. **Trace** the letters. **Write** the letters.

g g _ _   c c _ _   k k _ _

r r _ _   h h _ _   l l _ _

2 **Use** the code to colour the picture.

Code

r = ●   b = ●

g = ●   o = ●

3 Follow the lines. Say the letter sounds. Blend the sounds to say the words. Write each word.

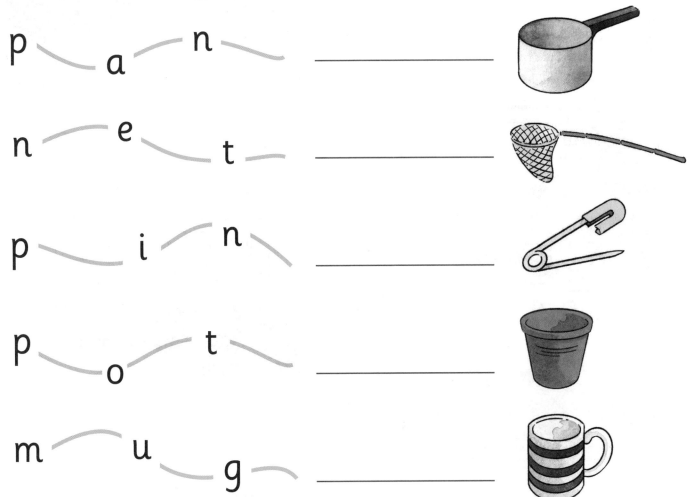

p　a　n　_____

n　e　t　_____

p　i　n　_____

p　o　t　_____

m　u　g　_____

4 Say the words. Which words rhyme? Circle the odd one out in each line.

➡ Mum　fun　run

➡ hop　got　top

➡ can　ran　bag

Have fun with nonsense words. Pretend to spot a made-up alien, e.g. *There's a grable on the…, there's a zug on the …* Ask your child to finish the sentence with a rhyming word, e.g. *table, rug.*

Try this!

Blending sounds

Why did the family run after the bus?

1 **Retell** the story.
Circle the right word in each caption.

Mum left the bag / bog.

The bus set on / off.

The dog run / ran.

The bus did stop / hop.

Mum was sad / glad.

2 **Choose** the right stickers to label the picture.

Try this!

Talk like a robot. Say a three-letter word, but break it up into its different letter sounds, e.g. *c-a-t*. Ask your child which word the 'robot' is trying to say.

Two letters, one sound

How did Mum feel when she got her bag back?

1 Sometimes two letters make one sound. **Read** the words. **Circle** the two letters in each word that make one sound.

duck   doll   sock   clock

bell   Biff   hill   puff

2 **Say** the sounds of the letters in the cloud. **Join** the pictures to the letters that each word ends with.

ck   ll   ff

24

3 **Follow** the dotted lines. **Say** the sounds. **Write** the words.

b a ck _____

s o ck _____

B i ff _____

h i ll _____

b e ll _____

Spelling words

Have you ever lost anything important? What did you do?

1 **Look** at the pictures. **Say** the words. **Write** the words.

b_____

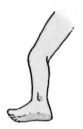

l_____

h_____

d_____

b_____

c_____

r_____

D_____

10

t_____

2 **Look** at the pictures. **Write** the words.

_____

_____

_____

_____

_____

Try this! Play the robot game from page 23. This time ask your child to be the robot and sound-talk a word for you to guess.

27

Writing words

Have you been on a bus journey? Where did you go?

Which of these things do you think Mum had in her bag? **Find** stickers for the missing objects. **Say** the words. **Write** the missing words.

pin

__ __ __

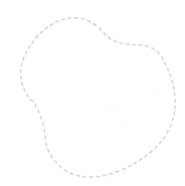

bell

__ __ __

tag

__ __ __

28

a b c d e f g h i j k l m

_ _ _ _   _ _ _ _   bug

map   _ _ _ _   _ _ _ _

_ _ _ _   laptop   _ _ _ _

Try this!

Choose one letter. Form it in different ways, e.g. draw it in chalk, make it out of sticks or stones, paint it, make it out of food, write it in bubbles in the bath, air write it.

n o p q r s t u v w x y z

29

common and tricky words

Read the stories again. Talk about the common words that appear more than once. Some of these are tricky to read.

1 **Say** the letter sounds. **Blend** the sounds to read the words. **Circle** the words you can read.

off

get

mum

got

on

back

is

and

dad

2 **Write** the missing words from the puzzle pieces.

Dad ____ wet.    **is**

Mum got ____ .    **Dad**

Mum ____ off.    **got**

Mum ____ Dad ran.    **and**

3 These are tricky words. **Say** the words.
Add a star sticker for each word that you know.

go ☆   the ☆   to ☆   no ☆

was ☆   my ☆   her ☆   that ☆

4 **Read** the rhyme. **Draw** a circle around the tricky words.

Go, Chip, go!

To the top.

Huff and puff.

Do not stop!

Try this!

Tricky words contain one or two letters that do not match the sounds that your child has learned so far. The best way to learn to read tricky words is to practise until your child recognises them. Make your own flashcards by writing tricky words on pieces of scrap cardboard. Keep them in your bag or pocket to look at on the bus or in a queue.

Well done!

_____

has completed the

Stories and Activities

Date _____ , 20 _____

OXFORD
UNIVERSITY PRESS

Great Clarendon Street, Oxford, OX2 6DP, United Kingdom

Oxford University Press is a department of the University of Oxford. It furthers the University's objective of excellence in research, scholarship, and education by publishing worldwide. Oxford is a registered trade mark of Oxford University Press in the UK and in certain other countries

Activity pages text © Oxford University Press 2018

Get Dad!, The Bag on the Bus text © Roderick Hunt 2006, 2014

Get Dad! illustrations © Alex Brychta 2006
The Bag on the Bus illustrations © Nick Schon 2014

Get Dad! first published in 2006
The Bag on the Bus first published in 2014

The characters in this work are the original creation of Roderick Hunt and Alex Brychta who retain copyright in the characters.

Activities written by Isabel Thomas

The moral rights of the author have been asserted

First published in 2018

British Library Cataloguing in Publication Data
Data available

ISBN: 978-0-19-276458-4

10 9 8 7 6 5 4 3 2

Paper used in the production of this book is a natural, recyclable product made from wood grown in sustainable forests. The manufacturing process conforms to the environmental regulations of the country of origin.

Printed and bound in Great Britain by Bell and Bain Ltd, Glasgow

Acknowledgements

Series Editor: Annemarie Young
Activity pages additional artwork by Stuart Trotter